Teamwork in Equine Assisted Teams

© 2016 Ilka Parent/Minds-n-Motion

Interested in hosting an experiential, equine assisted "Teamwork in Equine Assisted Teams" workshop?

Contact me for more information:

Ilka.parent@mindsnmotion.net

Disclaimer

The information provided in this publication is for general informational purposes only. All activities involving horses have inherent risks, including danger to body and limb. Any individuals who wish to participate in equine-assisted psychotherapy should do so only under appropriate psychotherapeutic care. Any practitioners who wish to participate in equine assisted psychotherapy should do so only after receiving appropriate training in either the mental health profession or equine biology. The author does not make any representations or warranties as to the information in this publication and expressly disclaims any and all liability arising out of participation in or utilization of any techniques, experiences or activities involving horses.

Teamwork in Equine Assisted Teams

DEDICATION

I am dedicating this manual
to my son, my daughter,
and my three horses
Monte, Lance and Amin –
Two- and Four-Leggers
who mean the world to me.

CONTENTS

Teamwork in Equine Assisted Teams

ACKNOWLEDGMENTS

My "Thank You" goes out to all former and present equine
assisted team members – both Two- and Four-legged Ones! All of
you have made it possible to provide high quality care to people
who deserve the best.

1. Introduction to the first edition (2013)

It seems like it was ages ago – and it certainly has been several teams ago – that I started working with the EAGALA model. Even though it's been a time filled with an array of new impressions, people and experiences, I will never forget a scene from the very beginning. I was contracted by a therapist as an Equine Specialist. We were working with young children during an Easter camp. I hadn't attended an "Un-Training" yet. "My" therapist had explained the model to me, but it would be an overstatement to say I had a clue about what I was supposed to do. The children with whom we were working all had a history of sexual abuse. As the Equine Specialist, I was keeping a close eye on the horses, but the kids were hyper, there were a lot of them, and the horses were very agitated and even aggressive not only towards the other horses, but also the children. I didn't know about the category of Apostrophe S yet, but at this point, my counter transference was all over the place.

Despite this rather negative experience, I attended my first EAGALA training a little over 10 years ago. Back then, Mark Lytle and Lynn Thomas were my trainers. I listened, I didn't understand. Somehow I was fascinated, even though I was lacking structure and theory. I listened and watched some more. During one of the breaks, I approached Mark and described the situation from camp. I expected safety instructions, guidelines, or some form of advice. His answer threw me. He said, "Have you looked at your relationship with your therapist?"

That was my introduction to the team aspect of working with the EAGALA model.

Since then, I have had the pleasure, discomfort, stress and joy of working on and with various teams who implemented the EAGALA model into their work. Having been part of a military community means that friends and coworkers, including myself, move and change a lot. "Teamwork" is probably a concept that a number of you readers have dealt with as facilitators: Equine Assisted Learning is often offered to help organizations and teams improve. But as far as our own team is concerned, I believe that our work involves having to be more vulnerable than regular teams. We are, or are supposed to be, aware of our own contributions, our filters, our so-called Apostrophe S. In our equine assisted work, we learn about one another on deeper levels. That vulnerability within the team is good, but it also makes the possibility of developing team conflict much greater.

This handbook is a reflection on and a collection of my experiences, as well as what I use and have used to enhance teamwork in our team. The focus is on two areas. The first addresses general ways to improve your teamwork – technical tips and tricks, so to speak. Whether you are just starting out or have worked together for a long time, paying attention to these areas will help minimize your effect on the interaction between clients and horses. The second section looks at typical issues that can arise, especially in equine assisted teams.

Over the years, in our team, we have learned to take whatever issues we have to the horses. Who better to help us than our equine team members? However, I have no intention of providing you with a step-by-step guideline or instructional booklet. My hope is that by presenting different issues from both the Mental Health Specialist's and Equine Specialist's perspectives, and by providing examples that relate to or indicate problem areas, this manual will assist you in individually formatting what meets YOUR needs. In other words, I am inviting you to set your stage: I am providing you with a framework and have added some props you might consider using. In some of my writing I might be a bit more directive, but overall I have no clue as to what your story is. I would like to invite you to explore what may or may not help improve your own teamwork!

Germany, September 2013

Ilka Parent with

the Minds-n-Motion Team

2. Introduction to the second edition (2016)

During my research for and the writing of my recently published book, *The Fundamentals of Equine Assisted Trauma Therapy* (2016), I realized that my understanding of the teamwork in Equine Assisted Teams has changed over the past three years, which is when I originally wrote this manual. I decided to change, or rather to expand and update it to reflect my current understanding.

Even though it is hard not to correct style and language, the main body remains the same as it was three years ago. There are a few changes and additions: First of all, I have expanded the audience for whom this handbook is intended. There has been a surge in interest and application of ground based equine assisted work throughout the world. EAGALA has achieved a tremendous task in making equine assisted therapy popular. However, where it only used to be EAGALA and PATH as certifying leaders in this market, there are now numerous organizations who offer certification in ground based equine assisted therapy, equine assisted coaching, equine assisted professional development, and so on. All of them are focused on not offering any riding, and most of them have adapted the standard of working in a team. Therefore, this handbook is still written for Equine Specialists and the Mental Health Specialists alike who work together on a team with horses on the ground, in an effort to provide equine assisted work to clients. But I have changed the title from "Teamwork in EAGALA Teams" to "Teamwork in Equine Assisted Teams".

The biggest addition to the old handbook involves a formal description of the roles and responsibilities of each team member. Even though each certifying organization has different opinions of the horses' roles and responsibilities, the human team members' parts seem to be consistent throughout, making it possible to provide a description without favoring any organization or model.

One major change, even though the attentive reader did read it in the original handbook, is the emphasis on the well-being and the role of the horses. It has come to my attention that not everybody shares the same outlook on the ethical aspect of working with these wonderful animals, and I have taken the liberty to share my viewpoint on this issue in a more outspoken and direct manner.

But why a book on teamwork in equine assisted teams at all? Even though we all know it, let me spell it out. Conflicts within our team can have disastrous effects on our clients, on us, and also on our horses. Good team members are too expensive and too valuable to lose. I can not afford to get a new horse or new team member every time there is a conflict. In my experience, equine assisted work, when done correctly, is intense, fulfilling, challenging, heart breaking, heartwarming, awe invoking, humbling, overwhelming and absolutely awesome. Internal conflicts and stressors added to an already intense work are the perfect breeding ground for disagreements and future dissolution. Yet, in my experience, there are several things we can do to prevent this from happening.

This book was written with the intent to address the main issues that may arise when working in a team in Equine Assisted Work; a book honoring the different perspectives of the therapist, as well as of the equine specialist. And, as is my style, a handbook written for both therapists and equine specialists. In a way, it is a personal handbook – personal opinions from both perspectives are expressed, at times with humor, at times with criticism, at times with sarcasm. Definitely not a textbook, although there are a couple of references to books from which quotes were taken. Hopefully a handbook that is useable and easy to read, and yet thought provoking.

The handbook starts with a few paragraphs about teamwork in equine assisted work. The ethical aspects of working with horses as equal team members, while subjecting them to people who, at times, suffer from psychological disorders, will be addressed. The areas of responsibility and scopes of function of each team member involved will be differentiated and explained. Following this background information, typical issues are addressed from different perspectives, and some tips and tricks are presented to help raise the awareness of potential team conflicts.

While this handbook is not a step-by-step manual, the concepts provided can be applied and modified to meet individual requirements. This handbook caters to the demands to describe perspectives in such a way that they can be related to and hopefully used in your practice. However, it needs to be stressed that no experientially based concepts can be learned from textbooks. This handbook neither claims exclusivity nor inclusivity. Ethically accepted practices require that expert knowledge is individually formatted to meet clients' needs – and in this case, it is you and your team members who are your own "clients".

This handbook was not designed and thought of at a desk; nor was it copied from anybody. Rather it is the accumulated experience over the past decade that, at times, was painfully gained in my own practical work. It hopes to address and verbalize things we typically do not talk about. It also is again a way for me to continue to share my passion of attempting to make it possible for people and teams to deliver ethically and clinically great care to people in need.

Even though, in this day and age, gender neutrality is important, the following text will refer to individuals as "he" and "him". This is a purely stylistic convention and implies no gender specific bias.

Obermohr, Germany, July 2016

Ilka Parent

3. Teamwork is.... Selected Quotes

"The most special part/aspects/characteristic about our equine assisted/EAGALA team is

_____?" June 2013

- "That we finish well"

- "Cohesiveness and being dean with each other"

- "Understanding each other's Apostrophe S"

- "Mutual respect and dedication to learn more about each other's roles"

- "Reading each other's mind, trusting each other and the process, communicating without words"

- "The way we intuitively cooperate and listen to each other without saying a word"

- "...the horses - they always keep it real"

- "The openness we share in our team dialogue which helps to deepen the understanding and creativity in the experience in the session with dients and horses."

- "The fun we have working together, outside, with horses."

- "The comfort of not being alone, no matter what."

"The most special part/aspects/characteristic about our equine assisted/EAGALA team is _____?" June 2016
• "....is our connectedness with one another which gives us the ability to work in a very fluid and free flowing synchronistic way. As a team we unanimously agree that the horses are the expert members of the team so we always pay attention to what they are showing us!" • "....is our comfort/trust level we have with each other to concentrate on our own job of providing the very best support for the client...trusting the wisdom of the main team member the horse." • "The professionalism and trust in the arena/pasture/field and the ability to talk, laugh and relax outside it." • "The unspoken connection and trust between two and four legged members." • "The unwavering truth that is present with the horses and whoever the team is....one's own junk even comes out..." • "Trust & support. The trust in the horses to evoke what needs to be explored by the client. The support of a colleague to create space for self-reflection." • "Connection and Trust The Process!" • "The most special aspect about the EAGALA team I am working on is the openness and trust. 1 + 1 does not equal 2 – together as a team we become something more, wiser and more knowledgeable. It is like a dancing team – we both follow and lead each other."

Table 1: Quotes about Equine Assisted Teamwork

4. Theoretical Background

Even though from a teaching perspective, one should never start with mentioning something that it is NOT, I would like to state first what this handbook is not about:

Several years ago it seemed rather easy to decide on which model to pick when one wanted to work with horses and people: There were only two major organizations who certified and/or provided certification in Equine Assisted Psychotherapy and Learning.

Several years later it is no longer that easy. To date, there is no independent certification in Equine Assisted Psychotherapy or Equine Assisted Learning and Professional Development that is *required* by any public jurisdiction, or monitored by any *independent* organization. Now there are numerous organizations that will certify individuals interested in equine assisted work. Each one claims high professionalism and worldwide standards. Certification requirements vary by organization and country.

The confusion for anybody interested in this field does not stop there: one needs to decide whether one wants to do regular psychotherapy, counseling, organizational work, or coaching with horses. Some institutions say riding is helpful, others insist it is not. Some speak of horses mirroring people, others insist they do not. Some say that horses are spiritual beings, able to detect more in humans than humans are capable of, others refer to pure biology.

All of the above topics and discussions resulting therefrom are not subject of this handbook.

4.1.Equine Assisted Models and Teamwork

What most certifying organizations in equine assisted work insist on is a team approach, meaning at least two individuals work together with at least one horse, in an effort to provide equine assisted interventions. One is typically a person who knows horses and horse behaviors, the other a person who knows humans and human behaviors. Every time there are two or more individuals working together, you have a team.

If you take a theoretical excursion, much literature can be found on teamwork. Various authors take turns coming up with new and/or easier concepts, solutions and theories. Throughout it all, it appears to be easier to define dysfunctional teams rather than functional ones. Commonly identified factors in teams that are not working well together are "absence of trust", "different conflict resolution skills", "lack of commitment", "lack of accountability", "different outlooks/priorities", "competition", "lack of communication" and "different personality styles", just to list a few.

Typical solutions offered to resolve or prevent such issues are team meetings, rope courses, profiling and conflict analysis. Recommended readings are definitely the works by Patrick Lencioni[1]; however, most of them are theoretical and all consist of classroom teachings – something I am assuming we all steered away from when we became interested in Equine Assisted Work. So, no worries – I won't go into all the psychological aspects of team dysfunction!

---

[1] Patrick Lencioni (2002):"The Five Dysfunctions of a Team"

4.2.Cooperation within the Team

Equine Assisted Work requires the combination and collaboration of three competencies. To my knowledge, there is not one person who has enough knowledge to come even close to the knowledge that three team members can bring in. One person alone is not capable of fulfilling all areas of responsibility that should be distributed among team members. However, when there are at least two team members, stepping over boundaries into another team member's area of responsibility can happen and, typically, has a negative impact on the overall process. All team members need to collaborate and cooperate with each other. The meeting of such very different work areas means that concepts and guidelines out of all areas need to be respected and utilized effectively by all. That does not mean that therapists need to become equine specialists, or equine specialists need to become coaches, or either two-legged team members need to become a horse. A horse???

What is most unusual about equine assisted work when adhering to a team approach is that sessions are *always* facilitated by a team consisting of at least two people and at least one horse. Each horse is respected as a sentient being and an equal team member. Each team member has specific functions within the team and specific areas of responsibility within the teamwork. Depending on the nature of the equine assisted work, the team consists of one or more horses, a person who knows horses and horse behaviors, and a specialist for people, e.g. a psychotherapist, a therapist, a counselor, a coach, an educator, a consultant, etc. Several years ago I started referring to the different members on our team as "two-legged" and "four-legged" team members. This terminology is widely used in the German language to refer to animals as is, and it just seemed fitting to avoid a differentiation between human and equine team members. I have been told that is does not translate well into various languages, but in German and English it seems to work and our clients have taken well to this.

4.3. Instrumentalizing Horses (Blog: Minds-n-Motion)

When we introduce new clients to our work, we stress that horses are not "instrumentalized". Our work developed out of working with what is commonly known as the EAGALA model: We work in a team, we do not offer any riding, our work is solution oriented – and we thought we adhered to the EAGALA code of ethics. Very early on, EAGALA took it upon themselves to address the horses' well-being in their ethical codex. Paragraph 2 of the EAGALA ethics codex states:

§2: "The EAGALA associate will respect and honor the value and dignity of all and protect the safety, welfare, and best interests of clients and horses."[2]

As it turns out, we seem to have expanded our under-standing: by simply referring to the horses as four legged team members on our team, we inadvertently changed and expressed our perception of them: we made them equal, meaning that the horses on our team are not put into situations into which we would not put ourselves. Just like us, they have a choice. This viewpoint is difficult to

implement and adhere to at times, as we will see in later parts. However, we do not put our horses in situations

they themselves would not choose to be in, which is the main

[2] EAGALA ethics codex, paragraph 2,
http://www.eagala.org/sites/default/files/attachments/EAGALA%20Code%20of%20Ethics_1.pdf (June 2016)

reason why we do not offer any riding.

Of course a definition like that can not be made universal and depends largely on an individual's experience, point of view and general attitude. My view changed because over the years I witnessed situations where horses did not want to be part of any therapeutic or professional developmental process. Much to my dismay, I myself was in situations, working as an Equine Specialists, where horses definitely did not want to be part of the process and where it was not in their best interest to have them there. It created a conflict: wanting to cooperate with my team mate, the mental health specialist, wanting to get paid for my work by the attending team, not being sure if it was my "own stuff" that was creating the problem, and really not wanting to subject my horses to a situation in which they were not safe.

I have also been in situations where horses were labeled with metaphors and thus were "instrumentalized". After the sessions, these horses who did great for the clients were colicking or continued to show signs of stress for several hours. I have seen horses with ropes and halters, tied down and being restricted in their freedom during a single "exercise". I have seen horses with groups of more than 60 people, seemingly completely overwhelmed by the sheer number of people, with no means to escape.

All of these situations led to the above realization and shift. Horses are sentient beings with the right to choose. In our "job description" for horses, they are entitled and encouraged to be horses. Our standard of whom we work with is pretty high, but the horses typically pass our criteria in the first round, as they know how to be authentic and horses. It is OUR responsibility to watch out that they are not harmed, overwhelmed or stressed in our work –

meaning, we do not use them as tools, make them something they are not, or keep them in situations where they have no choice.

In other words, we very, very rarely use ropes. Or halters. We do not allow for clients to tie them to anything. We typically work in large fields, where horses have a choice to join or stay away. We let the horses choose which person they want to work with. We, or rather the Equine Specialists on our team, watch out for their safety and health, meaning that we do at times take horses out of the process. As they do not verbalize what they are experiencing, it is our responsibility to have enough horse knowledge to be able to look out for them. We implement steps and follow guidelines that make it possible for our horses to act in their best interest. They are equal members of our team and, to us, they have the same choices, rights, needs and wishes as we humans do. That is our understanding of "not instrumentalizing" the horses.

4.4.Allocation of Responsibilities in the Team

Based on what has been explained so far, the following "job descriptions" are easy to understand and are self-explanatory. As mentioned in the introduction, only the areas of responsibility and scopes of expertise of ground based teamwork will be focused on. Each role has varying demands in terms of training, preparation, and opportunities for credentialing with various organizations. Some organizations train and certify for dual roles, some do not. Some of the following paragraphs were taken directly out of the book *The Fundamentals of Equine Assisted Trauma Therapy.*

4.4.1. The Horses' Job Description

During the interaction with clients, horses are given as much room as possible. It is up to them to "be horses", and to have free choice whether they want to interact with humans or not. This is a safety aspect: by providing the room for horses to remain horses, they have the opportunity to flee. Utilizing restrictive training aids, such as halters and lead ropes, is advised against. A tied down horse no longer has the ability to flee.

Participating horses are not to be instrumentalized. Participating clients are not taught or lectured about horse training techniques or horse specifics. This, at first, may appear contradictory or dangerous. However, as there is no objective for the horses to meet, there is no right or wrong way for them to be. In all equine assisted work, horses are able to act and react according to their needs and their nature.

4.4.2. The Equine Specialist's Job Description

Equine specialists, also called "ES", counsel and advise "their" human teammates on properly selecting participating horses. According to their expertise on the physical and psychological demands on the horses, they decide on the space in which the interaction with clients will take place. It is the equine specialist's expert knowledge about horse-specific behaviors that is essential for ensuring the physical safety of all involved. That includes the right to decide about the duration of the horses' participation. It is possible for horses to experience stress through the interaction, rendering them unsuitable for this type of work. Equine specialists watch out for the physical and psychological demands on the horses. They are responsible for the horses appropriate care before and after each session. Equine Specialists should have many years of in-depth horse experience working with many different horses in many different settings. Profound knowledge and expertise in being able to read equine behaviors and herd dynamics even in unusual circumstances should be a prerequisite for any certification in this field.

If working with the EAGALA model, the horses' behavior during the interaction with clients is observed and categorized according to specific observational categories. Equine specialists observe how the horses' behaviors and dynamics change during the horse-human interaction among and between them. They also take note of possible horse reactions to participants. They share their observations with the therapist.

Equine specialists support clients in and during the process of becoming aware of their experiences with the horses. They support processing by providing observations based on the horses' behaviors, utilizing special techniques that vary depending on the certifying organization Building on the horse observations and adhering to the agreed upon treatment plan or contract, both equine specialist and human team mate design the follow up activities that encourage and support the client in the agreed upon process.

4.4.3. The Therapist's/Counselor's Job Description

Psychotherapy is a protected term which can only be used by individuals who have the training and license to practice in their country and respective state. Licensing requirements vary by country and by State. E.g. in the United States of America, licensed mental health therapists may be Social Workers, Psychologists, Counselors, and Marriage & Family Therapists. Licensed therapists are mental health care providers, trained in the assessment and treatment of mental disorders as described in the DSM-V; and obligated to maintain current competence in the mental health field.

According to the agreed upon treatment goals, the therapist's main duties are to accompany and assist individuals seeking help in their process to gain insight and decrease clinical symptoms. Therapists, also called mental health professionals (MH), follow certain paradigmatic concepts and models they have learned during their clinical training. Instead of talking about topics, processing is encouraged through experiential activities with horses. Depending on the equine assisted model with which they are working, the therapist focuses on the clients' nonverbal communication, utilized symbols and potential metaphors. Relevant subjects are reflected and then taken up in follow up activities. When designing activities, the equine specialists' horse observation are considered and integrated. Overall, the therapist ensures the emotional safety of all involved - including treatment team members.

4.4.4. Educators, Coaches, Consultants

Educators, coaches and consultants come from a wide variety of backgrounds. Some have formal certification such as an advanced degrees and/or teaching certificates, some are psychologists who have focused on working with organizations. For simplicity, they will be grouped under "MH" as well. Educators design and guide learning for individuals or groups, based on principles that have proven relevant to the particular group being served. Similar to the therapist, they are responsible to stay focused on agreed upon learning goals and contractual agreements. Their main duty is to accompany and to assist individuals seeking new insights in their process of learning new skills. Educators, coaches and consultants follow certain paradigmatic concepts and learning models they have learned during their training. Instead of talking about topics, processing is encouraged through experiential activities with horses. Depending on the equine assisted model with which they are working, they focus on the clients' nonverbal communication, utilized symbols and potential metaphors. Relevant subjects are reflected and then taken up in follow up activities. When designing activities, the equine specialists' horse observation are considered and integrated. Overall, the educator, coach and/or consultant ensures the emotional safety of all involved, meaning that therapeutic topics are to be avoided. Particularly when working with organizational teams, it is their responsibility that attending participants are able to return to work and their co-workers the next day without having shared or disclosed too much personal information during the equine assisted training.

4.4.5.   Is it Coaching or Therapy?
(Blair McKissock)

In the industry if equine assisted learning and therapy there is a great debate among professionals: what is the difference between learning and therapy? Having been a professional in experiential education for over 20 years, this was never an issue because each experience was therapeutic regardless of who was leading it and we were trained how to process an experience without being a therapist. For us there was a lane in which we stayed. We were not therapists but we knew how to keep the conversation in the context of experiential learning. More and more there is a growing grey area between the two, especially between coaching and therapy. Those who facilitate equine assisted psychotherapy or counseling are licensed and credentialed mental health professionals according to their state. Those that fall into the learning side of the gray middle area are usually coaches, educators, instructors, etc. We recreation therapists fall somewhere in the middle. If you are interested in either getting into equine assisted learning and therapy as a career or as a client, it is important to know the difference.

"The **Scope of Practice** describes the procedures, actions, and processes that a healthcare practitioner is permitted to undertake in keeping with the terms of their professional license."

Within any profession, there is a scope of work or scope of practice that is defined by their competencies and by and applicable governing organizations and in some instances the federal government. It is the job of the facilitators to operate within the scope of their work and do their best not to cross the lines while facilitating groups and individuals. Almost anyone could be trained to facilitate an EAL session focusing on meeting basic competencies within the domains of horse knowledge and experiential education. This represents a facilitator level of practice and would include working as a co-facilitator, equine specialist or lead facilitator for a learning based group with basic goals. Only those with training and credentials as a mental health professional can offer counseling, psychotherapy, mental health therapies, etc. For example, a professional trained and licensed as an educator could not be the lead facilitator in a mental health session. This would be beyond the scope of their work. But a licensed therapist would be the lead in a psychotherapy session.

The Difference between Coaching and Therapy

On the learning end of the spectrum, the coaching or self-growth model is usually followed. The coaching process differs from counseling in that counseling tends to focus on healing from past trauma and coaching focuses on the future through goal setting and accountability. Coaching also tends to focus on the development of basic life skills need to accomplish those goals. In the process of change, the horse can be the companion and even the guide. However, it can be helpful to have a coach serve as the navigator or interpreter. Coaches can often fill that role. You are the driver in the process of change, but, just as a horse asks questions during interaction such as "Are you going to be the leader?", a coach can help ask that one question that reveals a new personal insight that can be the key to reaching your personal goals. Coaches are not therapists. They don't process past trauma or past emotions. They do, however, help a client look to the future. A good coach would also be able to recognize when a client needs additional support from a mental health therapist and would make a referral. Because, in any session, things situations arise and people become emotional, it is critical that coaches have the necessary skills to keep any client safe, know their own emotional competencies and have the tools to keep the session in the learning lane and have appropriate back up.

Therapy, on the other hand, looks much different. A therapist first of all is someone who has received an education, then training and supervision, taken a board exam, and has been then licensed in their state as a mental health professional. There are several avenues the professional can take to licensure. They range from licensed clinical social worker, licensed practicing counselor, mental health counselor, marriage and family therapist, clinical psychologist, and an addictions counselor. Only those credentialed as a mental health professional can legally offer mental health services. In their work, they tend to focus on processing past trauma or working through a chronic mental health condition. Therapists are more flexible in that they can move into more coaching based methodologies but it all depends on what the client's goals are as to the qualifications necessary for the facilitator. Recreation therapists fall in the grey area in that they are qualified to lead mental health services including group therapy focused on the development of leisure and life skills inside a clinical setting but could not go into private practice as a mental health professional. In some states they are licensed.

It is very easy to cross the line from learning into therapy and in some cases that can be OK if the facilitator is a therapist. However, if the purpose of the session is a learning or coaching goal and the facilitator is not a licensed mental health professional he has to stay within the scope of his work. It is for the safety of everyone involved. In the end it is the ethical responsibility of both the consumer and the facilitator to do their due diligence. For consumers it is about doing their homework when investigating a potential therapist, coach or horse professional for equine assisted services. For the professionals it is about knowing their professional limits and staying in their lane. If they do not have the required competencies to meet the needs of a potential client, then they need to bring in a partner who does have those competencies or to seek out additional training. There are many certifications out that train people to facilitate equine assisted learning and therapy and there is a great disparity between the good ones and the not-so-good ones. In the end, professionals need to do their homework to before taking on the amazing responsibility of facilitating the healing relationship between humans and horses.

Blair McKissock MSEd RYT is a speaker and author on experiential and nature based learning. You can learn more about coaching, OmHorse mounted yoga sessions and upcoming equine assisted trainings at www.stridestosuccess.org.

4.5.Teamwork in the Team

What do we do in equine assisted work? As can be seen by the job descriptions, we attempt to facilitate a person's process by having them interact with horses in specifically designed activities. It makes sense to look at established learning models to understand what we do and why we do it. By being aware of how change in a person and learning can take place, and understanding what our job is in making that possible, we are one step further in making our team work well together.

David A. Kolb, an American professor for Organizational Psychology, and Roger Fry described 1975 how learning can take place when a person experiences something.

Teamwork in Equine Assisted Teams

In his meta-model, Kolb describes four learning steps:

1. Concrete experience
2. Observation and reflection
3. Generalization, conceptualization and abstract concept formation
4. Active analyzing, planning and renewed experimenting

Table 2: Kolb's Learning Model

If we take Kolb's learning model and look how interactions with horses fit into it, we come up with the following four steps:

1. In the first step, "concrete experience", a client has a practical and concrete experience with horses in the "Here and Now". The client receives direct feedback to his behavior through the horses' reaction.

2. In step two, reflection and observation takes place: when the client thinks and reflects about what happened during the human-horse interaction, it is possible for him to draw certain conclusions about what happened and to attach meaning to the experience. This either happens through self-reflection or through observations given by somebody else. In equine assisted interventions, these outside observations are typically provided by the equine specialist.

3. Reflection can lead to generalizations and concept formation. At the third stage, it is possible to generalize the concrete experience and to recognize underlying principles. Through conceptualizing, new knowledge can be transferred to other situations. It is part of the therapist's, educator's, coach's or consultant's responsibility to support the client in this process of conceptualization and possible transfer to every-day life.

4. The newly gained knowledge can now be practiced and tried out. The client can go home and apply it to day-to-day life; or he can plan and decide how to continue and to apply it in the here and now with the horses. The client is his own expert and can fully control what to do next.

Your scope of practice and theoretical orientation, be that teaching, counseling or clinical work, as well as the equine assisted model you have chosen to implement in your work affects the skills and techniques you use to facilitate these learning steps.

Being aware of what we are supposed to do does not mean that we are able to implement these steps perfectly. However, knowing about the above learning steps and being aware of one's area of responsibility already helps prevent crossing boundaries and stepping into team mates areas of responsibility.

5. Improve your Teamwork

As difficult as it may appear to fix bad teamwork, good teamwork can easily be recognized. It feels great when you and your team work well together, and everybody can spot it a mile away.

This handbook focuses on seven topics that are common in most teams: Our own nonverbal communication, shared values regarding professional demeanor, our own stuff, balance within the team, additional roles and responsibilities, communication and other typical areas of conflict. When addressed and openly discussed, your work within your team will improve.

5.1. Nonverbal Communication

5.1.1. Body Language and Positioning

Horses react to body language. That's why we work with them! Humans also pick up on body language – we are just not aware of it most of the time. If you browse through the literature on how much of our communication happens through our nonverbal communication, the percentage quoted on how much we communicate through it ranges from 70-90%. Even though that is a big span, no one will argue that it plays a big part in our day-to-day communication.

In Equine Assisted Work, we observe clients interacting with horses. However, the horses and clients will also react to our nonverbal communication!

Look at the following picture:

Picture used with permission from Sharon Boyce and Kristel Verhaegen, co-trainers at the Belgium EAGALA Part I training in August 2012.

This picture was taken at an EAGALA certification training that we had in Belgium in 2012. Sharon Boyce, Kristel Verhaegen and I were the EAGALA trainers at said training. When we first saw this picture, we couldn't help but laugh, but at the same time we wondered what interpretations might come up for others. Because, let's face it: Does it really look like we were in agreement with each other?

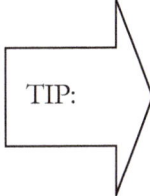

TIP: Videotaping your practice sessions or having pictures taken is a good way to sensitize you to your own body language.

Look at how all team members take the same leg position...

Another point that is important to mention is your position in regards to your team mates. Do you stay in proximity to your team members? "A good team stays together." Clinicians and practitioners familiar with group work might know this from working with clients: sometimes a team gets "split". The same applies to Equine Assisted Work – literally! A client will position himself between you and your human or equine team member. Another indicator for "non-togetherness" is when the team splits up without outside influences, e.g. when one team member moves closer to the client and the other stays back. Most of the time, we are not aware of this. Watch out for where you place yourself, help your team members identify any of those behaviors and raise your overall awareness to your nonverbal communication cues. If you find yourself separated from your team member, it is time for a check in!

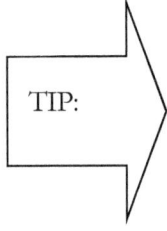

TIP:

A good exercise to practice staying together is for you and your teammates to hold a string or a rope of varying lengths between you. Make it long enough to allow for flexibility but short enough so that there will be tension if your team member leaves you during a "session". Try out different heights: one person kneeling, the other one standing up. Videotape yourselves and review it with your partner. Staying aware of your partner's body language keeps it in your mind that you DO have a partner. It may sound redundant, but this is a team approach with two *equal* humans working side by side. If one of you continually feels left out or out of place, it might be an indicator that there is an imbalance in your team.

5.1.2. Placement in the Arena.

"Typically, if you feel the need to step in, check in with your team member and take ten steps back." This is a sentence I often used in my EAGALA trainings. Even though there is no law that will tell you where to stand, over the years I have moved farther and farther away from the activity in the arena. I think this is where it depends on what population you work with and which competency field you are working in – MH or ES. From my clinical perspective, especially when I first started working with horses in a therapeutic setting, I was pinched countless times by a number of my Equine Specialists, urging me to step back and leave the experiential process to the clients. Check yourself. Why do you want to step in?

Do you need to hear more? Do you need to see more? Do you want to protect, help, or rescue your client? Are you worried that the desired and paid for outcome will not be reached? Check yourself to see what you are really paying attention to, and check in with your partner. If both the client's body language and the horses' behaviors indicate the need for you to intervene, then by all means do so – but make it an informed decision rather than an impulse. There needs to be a good (clinical) indication or compelling reason to facilitate a learning goal that warrants you stepping in.

Here is what one of our Equine Specialists said about her placement in the arena:

"Part of the ES's responsibility is to look out for the physical safety of our clients. We typically use the sentence, "We trust the fact that you will take care of your own safety," before clients start working with the horses. However, you still might encounter situations where the ES's perceived level of safety justifies stepping in. In this instance, the decision to step in is at the ES's discretion, based on his/her knowledge of horse behavior. Be aware that stepping in always disrupts the process the client is experiencing. Keep it to a minimum. Instead of screaming out "Stop," "Wow," or "Careful," a lot of times it is enough to consciously change your position in the arena. If you and your MH (whom you will notify – or take with you by the back of the arm) deliberately place yourselves in a different position, you might be able to diffuse a situation rather quickly. Let me give you an example. During one of our last trainings, all 15 participants were sitting in the arena on their chairs. They had placed their chairs in a circle on the short side of the arena, leaving a narrow pathway between themselves and the wall. At one point, the horses started running, and we were concerned that they might get trapped in that narrow area between the wall and the seats. However, simply moving ourselves closer to the entrance of the narrow pathway was enough to deter them from running through, as well as ease my concern for safety. The participants didn't even realize that we had intervened in a non-verbal way."

If a change in position is not enough, you can check in with the client in a way that is called "tracking." Tracking is when you provide a horse observation without expecting an answer or a conversation about it. It is a statement that is directed at no one, formulated in a neutral way, describing a scene or a picture that you, as Equine Specialist, want to draw attention to. For instance, we had a client who continuously placed herself behind horses, close to their hind quarters, in a spot where the horses did not see her. The client herself was unaware of this. She had no knowledge about horses. We were concerned for her safety in case one of the horses should turn around and step on her, but did not want to draw attention to only her. We were working with an entire group. So instead of coming in for a processing, the Equine Specialist "threw" the following horse observation out: "There are horses standing closely together with one person close to their behinds." Other participants started to look and pointed at the woman, and concerns were expressed by the group that it might not be "safe" for her to stand there where she could not be seen. Her behavior stopped without our having to intervene, and, at the same time, by having been given outside observations by other groups members, she had become aware of something she was doing that we could then follow up on in the group processing.

As one of our Equine Specialists put it:

"No matter how you decide to intervene, it is pertinent to communicate and be in agreement with your teammates. However, sometimes there is no time to explain what you are doing or to announce it to your team members: for instance, if the ES decides to take deliberate, directive action, it is absolutely necessary for his team member to support this decision. The Equine Specialist is responsible for the physical safety of all involved. Potential dangerous situations do not leave enough time to discuss pros and cons. If you as an ES can tell that a situation is potentially escalating, it is better to step in and intervene rather than letting it play out."

There are also other reasons why it is important to stay together until the client actually leaves the property. One of my ES's experienced the repercussions of not staying together pretty early on while working with a group of American soldiers afflicted by PTSD. At the end of the session, one of them literally "caught" her standing alone at the end of the arena. He started telling her about his experiences during his deployment, how they had affected him negatively in his life, and how much they still hurt him. It was some pretty bad stuff, and as she said later on, there are few other times she had felt this helpless. She felt conflicted: she did not want to be rude and not answer at all, but was also afraid to respond and possibly trigger something worse. She was convinced that a wrong utterance on her part might cause him to kill himself.

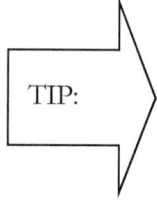

TIP:

Try standing in different locations around the arena and pay attention to the horses' focus as you move. Practice with a volunteer in the arena and take note of the changes when you move in closer or farther away. A good analogy is a camera zooming in and out. As you zoom in, some objects will be clearer while others on the outside of the perimeter will disappear. Once you zoom back out, however, all those objects come back into view and form a scene rather than a head shot. Ask yourself, why do you want to zoom in when you might miss things that are happening outside the frame?

5.1.3. Responsibility for our Team Members (Minds-n-Motion Blog)

If you read my recently published book *The Fundamentals of Equine Assisted Trauma Therapy* you read about collaboration and teamwork, roles and functions of team members, ways to facilitate sessions, and how to design activities with particular focus on working with traumatized military service members. You also read about why horses work particularly well in this setting, starting with their domestication, their abilities, their senses, their peculiarities and their specific roles in the "human-horse" interaction throughout medicine, psychology, mythology, history, and so on. In short, the book describes a methodological way of providing trauma therapeutic care to people suffering from PTSD.

You did not read about the effects of trauma on team members, two and four-leggers alike.

Several years ago we were facilitating one of our regular three day events for a group of service members with their partners. One of the partners had been diagnosed with complex PTSD. The group work was to focus and enhance relational skills, increase coping and symptom management skills. We were working with six clients in an oversized riding arena with four horses.

From the get-go, one of the horses showed very unusual behaviors: She kept running around, protecting one of the other horses - a horse she typically did not hang out with, even though all four are pastured together 24/7. We observed this for a while and, through horse observations, directed the clients' focus to it; but they did not have anything to say about this behavior nor could they relate to it. It got to the point where we decided to intervene for safety reasons. The horse was not endangering anybody, but she appeared to show signs of distress. We always mention in our introduction to new participants that we retain the right to take out horses at any time, being fully aware that such a change is an intervention by itself with potential consequences on the clients' process. But we were concerned about this horse. She was taken out and released. She was fine - no heavy breathing, no after sweating, no signs of distress.

We chose another horse, similar in build but different in personality, that also is pastured 24/7 with the horses that were working with the clients. The new horse immediately started to behave like the one we had just taken out; same behavior but different horse.

Obviously we checked in - paying even more attention to adhering to the facilitation skills I describe in detail in my book - and eventually one of the wives broke down in tears and related that this was exactly how she felt, wanting to protect her husband yet running herself into the ground.

To those of you who are experienced in Equine Assisted Psychotherapy, the following will not surprise: As soon as the wife starting talking about her real feelings, the new horse immediately slowed down and even lay down in the middle of the ring, next to one of the horses she had kept chasing away just moments before. She did not lay down because she was distressed. She did not lay down because she was exhausted. She was relaxed and awake. All the other horses lay down as well. The shift from agitation to relaxation was remarkable.

However, one of my Equine Specialists had turned around and had started crying. Seeing her horses in these conditions and hearing those stories were too overwhelming for her. At that moment she decided that she would no longer work with trauma clients. We still do other equine assisted work together, just not in the trauma field.

So the question: "Is it safe for the horses?" brings me back to all of our team members. As the MH on the team, I am responsible for the *emotional safety* of all team members – two- and four-legged ones. That means educating Equine Specialists on trauma and psycho-hygiene, and making sure that everybody is equipped with the proper tools and skills to be able to facilitate sessions within my scope of practice, and trusting my ES's to know about horses so that when they say "enough is enough", I will not argue.

Did I fail my team member in the situation described above? Yes, I did. It taught me a giant lesson on emotional safety and educating my team members on the specifics of our work.

5.2.Professional Demeanor

People sometimes assume that knowing how to interact with clients, whether from a clinical setting or a company, is simple and self-explanatory. It is not.

Clear guidelines regarding the expected professional demeanor in the setting you are working in, for all team members, are advisable. In a therapeutic environment, if working with specific populations or specific clinical disorders, it is important to be aware of certain clinical guidelines established by "your" clinician. In your work with organizations and companies, therapeutic talk is an absolute "no-go", and nobody wants to "go deep" if they are having to face their co-workers the next day again. Obviously, in every team, with any therapist, trainer or educator, there are variations. What is important is that your chosen guidelines fit your team and have been discussed and agreed upon by everybody involved – before you meet your clients! In my team, when conducting Equine Assisted Trauma Therapy, we all adhere to the clinical guidelines of psychoanalytically based psychotherapy. We do not share any personal information with our clients, not even about the horses. The session starts the moment our clients arrive, and does not end until they have driven away. This includes coffee and tea breaks as well! During that time, we focus on our clients and on the therapeutic goals and treatment plan we are following. We have clear role descriptions and clearly formulated expectations. During sessions, we communicate with each other – a lot! – about the process, so we know what stands out to each of us before we check in with our clients. Disagreements are discussed after the sessions when there are no clients nearby.

If you compare that with our professional development trainings, it is an entirely different picture! During those trainings we do not leave anything to chance: Depending on the size of the group coming out, we have up to eight team members, not counting the horses. Every team member is focused on making sure that the agreed upon "learning goal" is within reach to all participants in the tight schedule we typically have. Every team member knows what to do, at what time, and with whom: it is like a finely tuned machine that has been tuned up and prepared well in advance for the big event.

No matter what setting you are working in, it has proven advantageous to have a plan and a strategy put into place before clients come to you. Even if it sounds like this is very simple, it helps to have talked about it in your team and agreed who will do what before any clients show up.

5.3.Less is More

Have you ever had your session turn into talk therapy with horses grazing nearby? It makes for a nice atmosphere, but it has nothing to do with Equine Assisted Psychotherapy or Equine Assisted Learning. How about finding your equine team members literally between you and "your" client, or even treading on your toes? I once had a pony physically push me away -- from "MY" client!

A good example I like to bring up is a session where we were processing with a group of soldiers. This example does not show me in a favorable light, but it taught me an important lesson. The soldiers all carried raw eggs on spoons as their handicap. We had brought the eggs as symbols representative of their reported handicaps. They were carrying the eggs on spoons throughout the day. At one point, we'd been talking for a while, when one of our ponies walked up and started sniffing the eggs. One egg fell off the spoon - but to everybody's surprise didn't break! The pony started pushing the egg in the sand. The egg still didn't break! It took several minutes for this particular egg to break, and wasn't until the pony started nudging it around on the ground and finally bit it. Meanwhile, I was so wrapped up in processing that I heard myself say, "Let's just focus back on what we are talking about." Luckily, both my ES and I noticed my mistake. She stepped in and redirected everyone's attention to the horse's behavior, which gave us the opportunity to step away and leave our clients room to go back to what was important to *them*. This was a big lesson for me! Even though it greatly depends on the setting in which you work and the clientele with whom you work, I now have some sessions where neither I nor the ES ask a single question.

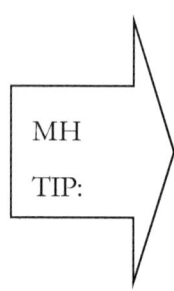

MH TIP:

One helpful tip is to set a limit for the "allowed" number of questions one may ask during processing and to keep that same number of pebbles, for example, in your pocket. Remove one pebble per question you ask. When all of them are gone, you have run out of allowed questions. Again, there is no "right" or "wrong" number of questions. Just practice and become more aware of how much you are speaking while processing and/or asking.

As one of our Equine Specialists put it:

"Especially during processing, the ES continues to observe the horses and their behaviors. It becomes pretty obvious when there is too much talking going on. The horses either step in between clients and team or disengage. The latter should be signaled to your MH, even though sometimes there really are situations when the conversation taking place is a clinical intervention."

Because physical safety is the ES's responsibility, the ES must have the room and right to intervene to ensure this physical safety when necessary. The emotional safety is the MH'S responsibility. Sometimes it is necessary to process something, even if the horses' behaviors indicate something else. When starting fresh in equine assisted work, MHs typically over talk. Initially, it is better to speak far less. Sound clinical judgement should determine when issues can be worked on experientially with the horses or verbally processed.

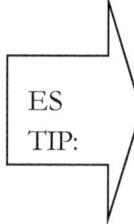

ES TIP:

Even during processing, the ES keeps an eye on the horses. It is really amazing how much the horses' continues to "reflect" what is being talked about. Yes, it is tempting to follow the conversation and get wrapped up in it, but even during processing, the client's process is not done. Although the activity is finished and everyone is "just talking", the horses still *react* to all humans in the arena, thus providing the ES with pertinent information about what may or may not be going on. The process is only really over when the client has left the property. Sometimes, when the flow of things has stopped, an ES might feel the urge to say something and break the silence. In those situations, it helps to focus on the horses instead. Sharing a horse observation can take the awkwardness away, reduce the pressure on the client, and can take the process in a new direction."

5.4.Balance

Most insecurities a team may experience will be seen or felt during the processing.

Each member of your team has his area of expertise, place and function. Unfortunately, many certifying organizations place an inequality on the team members: there are some who try to teach Equine Specialists how to be a counselor/therapist – and there are others who want the counselors/therapists to be equine specialists. As much as I believe that it is beneficial to all team members to know some of the principles the others work by, to me it is a relief not to have to know more than my own area of expertise. The team approach is chosen because each team member brings in special qualities, knowledge, and strength that amplifies and multiplies what can be offered. Some organizations let their participants experience the importance of their team members during the certifying courses: EAGALA, for instance, invites the MH's in the Part II training to be blindfolded and to listen to their

ES team mates share only horse observations about the client-horse interaction. One of its purposes is for each team member to experience the importance and expertise of the other: The Mental Health specialist experiences the importance of the Equine Specialist's observations, the Equine Specialist experiences metaphors based on horse observations, and the horses are able to do their jobs unperturbed! During our treatment team meetings, we have experimented with the Equine Specialists wearing earplugs. We found out, by coincidence, while working with Armed Forces members from international countries, that the ES's horse observations were far more detailed and accurate when the ES could not understand the soldiers' language.

Especially newly certified teams working with the principles of the EAGALA model and utilizing their observational categories (SPUDS) struggle with processing. Looking back at Kolb's learning model, processing is the part where horse observations are provided to the clients so that they can reflect on their experience. At some point the MH assists the client in generalizing their experience to where a transfer of what was experienced back into their life can be done. One of the questions I most often hear from teams is: "How do I know which question to ask or which horse observation to share?"

Of course, there are certain skills and techniques that each certifying organization teaches. In addition to those, for lack of a better example, I compare processing to going fishing. Please be aware that I don't even eat fish, but it's the picture that works for me:

Before I know where to go and where to cast my nets, I need to know where there are fish. In our team, it is the ES who first checks in with a very general question such as: "How did that go?" The client's answer indicates where there are possible fish waiting to be caught. Listening to what the client shares indicates where his attention during the experience was. His answer narrows the focus down to a specific time frame. The ES then casts out the so-called "fishing net," which is one or more questions based on the observed horse observation related to or in the vicinity of what the client just shared with us. The aim of those questions is truly to find out what the client perceived. If the client is unaware of a horse observation given by the ES, it truly does not matter!

Only when the client's answers provide enough material that are relevant to the clinician/consultant/coach, will the MH step in to ask further questions. If we stick with the fishing example, the ES's questions are the ever narrowing net around the fish and the MH question is the attempt to set the hook.

As one of our ES's shared a few years ago:

"What helped me as a "fresh" ES was the constant verbal exchange with my team members during sessions. We shared horse observations (loud enough to hear yet quiet enough to not disturb the clients and/or horses), wrote down the main SPUD'S, and, before checking in with the client, agreed on three to four top SPUD'S. When I felt most insecure, I also pre-formulated the questions with the help of my MH to ensure they were clean and judgment-free. This checking in with my MH helped me gain the confidence and safety I needed in order to work with real clients. Even if I made a blunder in my questions, I always knew I could rely on my MH to jump in and either redirect the question or distract from it. What is most important in all of this, however, is not to ever disagree, correct or criticize each other in front of your clients! I always knew I could fall back on my MH without worrying she would embarrass me. This confidence helped me tremendously as I grew into the role of ES. These days, we have clear roles and responsibilities; throwing out the fishing net and casting for fish is done without a second thought. We work within our capacities and really focus on our clients, which is what this work is really all about."

5.4.1. Parallel Process (Minds-n-Motion Blog)

When we enter the arena with our team members, we typically see one of two things happening: Everybody either takes his or her place and interacts with mutual respect, allowing for each team member to take their place and role without feelings of "being stepped on" or "tension in the air." We role model social interaction and conflict resolution. We add our knowledge, aiming to provide "quality care," with the main focus of meeting our clients' needs. We adhere to ethical standards, do not overstep each other's boundaries, and respect each other. We follow our chosen model's principles and model it in our teamwork. Or….

…..something completely different happens:

Disagreements. Typically, the equine specialists have been told to "keep quiet" because the therapists are the so-called "experts" on human behavior and know where to go clinically and pursue a subject. The therapists take the lead and pursue their goal – even if the horses are doing something completely different. If the equine specialist tries to interject, the mental health specialist takes it as an insult and will argue with psychological theories to prove his or her point.

….Most of the time, we are not aware or conscious of what we are feeling. That is why we use horses in this model!!! These feelings show up in our body language, the horses respond to that, and the

facilitators observe and point out the horses' behaviors. All this can lead to insights and awareness in our clients.

At this point parallel processes in sessions can occur. A parallel process is when the horses respond to the facilitators instead of the clients. Let me try to describe what happened in one of our trainings: we, as a trainer team, were facilitating a team of participants who were working with pretend clients. We ended up having four parallel processes going on at the same time:

The participants, pretending to be clients, felt split – they were not verbalizing their conflicts and claimed everything was all right. Tension appeared high among participants, and their body language reflected this.

The horses were in two separate groups, and when equine group members came close to each other, they showed their teeth.

The learning facilitators were split in two groups, with one member trying to speak and the others cutting her off.

The trainer team was discussing their own roles, as one team member had not spoken much that morning, and concerns were expressed about balance in the role modeling process.

What a classic example of parallel processes!

5.5. Emotional Involvement

I have been working with trauma clients for most of my professional life. I remember how I used to react when details and memories about sexual abuse, particularly during early childhood, were first shared with me. In the years of my training, supervision and mentoring, I learned to maintain neutrality, to shield myself, or, as I would like to put it, to change perspectives so that hearing those memories and seeing that pain does not frighten me any longer. I know that in the course of my work I have become accustomed to descriptions and shared events that are not considered "normal." Professionally, my focus is on what resources and skills help people overcome their trauma – which is an acquired change in my perception and is a tool that enables me to work with this population. And personally, I am absolutely certain that the person in front of me can overcome the traumatic experiences.

The typical Equine Specialist, on the other hand, usually has not had that type of training or exposure. I assume that in most equine assisted psychotherapy trainings, there is talk about confidentiality and emotional safety. I believe that emotional safety is something that extends to our team members – be it human or equine! Just as the Equine Specialist looks out for the horses' well-being, I occasionally check in with the human team members. This is something I always discuss and ask permission to do before we start working together. It needs to be agreed to by all parties involved! I check in if there are any emotional repercussions from or questions about a session. It is not my job, nor desire, to fix any team member's emotions, but it allows room for all of us to unload. Just as the horses need time with other horses to be fresh for new clients, we need time and space to be able to unload or refresh as well. As for myself, as any clinician I know, I have regular intervision and supervision. It is part of the so-called "psycho-hygiene". Even if you and your team are not working with psychiatric populations or trauma, it is the MH's area of responsibility to ensure the emotional safety within the team.

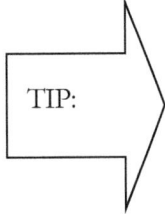

TIP:

One thing we implement on our team is something we coined "bird bath." Before each session, we share whatever is on our mind – our own stuff – and may have happened before we got to work. Then we put it away, like in an outside box. After each session, we take the time to "spill our stuff" and empty out whatever is still in the box or might have been added during the session to it: "gut impressions and reactions", self-contributions, disagreements, emotions – whatever it is that we kept away during the session. Our agreement is that nothing of what gets spilled during the bird bath is taken personally. The German writer Herman Hesse says, "It always changes a little once you have spoken it out loud." Once the "box" is emptied, we look to see what is our own stuff and what actually relates to our clients as in a potential parallel process that has taken place, or possible emotions being acted out by us instead of the clients, and…, and…, and…

The overall picture we use for this process is birds taking a bath in a fountain – getting wet, spilling water, shaking it off – without judgment.

As one of our ES's put it:

"Just as described above, in our therapeutic work I was confronted with things that go beyond my typical, everyday experience. Initially, I had to get used to having my MH persistently ask me if everything was okay or if I needed to talk about something. I am actually personally quite content that I don't know or don't get to know much about our clients' background and that I can't "read between the lines" like my MH does. I think all of us are different about

this stuff, but even before a session, I really don't want to know details about the client. What also helps me are the horses. I focus completely on them during our work, and I help support the process by asking well-timed horse observations. Everything else is my MH's area of responsibility. This clear and firm understanding of our areas of responsibility provides me with comfort."

Another ES on our team said once:

"The birdbath after each session, where we can get rid of everything we accumulate, is good, but usually I need a bit longer to be able to verbalize my impressions. My MH has gotten used to calling me a couple of days after a session, especially our three-day events, to check in with me. This is pretty close to perfect teamwork for me. We respect each other's differences and, if possible, accommodate them."

Here the comment of yet another ES on our team:

"Let's remember that our team doesn't only consist of two-legged members, but primarily of four-legged ones. Just as we humans deal differently with different situations, horses deal differently with the demands of these therapy sessions as well. I think the biggest mistake is to underestimate the work they do in these sessions and how much they carry. They perceive and take in all the emotions flying around in the arena – from the clients and/or the treatment team – and react to them. Whether they sense tension, aggression (covered or open), or something else, they register, respond, and show it in their own reactions. Some horses are quite capable of dealing with it all and want to do this work. We work at several different barns, and at each one of them the horses seem to recognize us. I only need to think of one of our Haflingers and one of our ponies. All of them get really excited when we come to the barn. They whinny, nicker, and seem very eager to get to the arena and start. But we've also had horses who were so sensitive that this type of work became a burden to them. Signs of stress can be nervousness, frequent elimination, stress yawning, and excessive sweating. I have seen horses show these stress signals even up to a day after sessions. Here it is the responsibility of the ES to speak for our four legged team members and to take them out of a session or even a program. Especially

during events or seminars that go on for several days, the ES has to make sure that the horses are not affected in a negative way or, if they are, make sure they are given proper time to recuperate. The well-being of our four-legged team members has top priority!"

Obviously, taking a horse out of a seminar or several day event is a very directive move. We are very aware of possible repercussions such a move can have for our clients and only do this if it is clearly indicated by our horses' physical and mental health. To prevent negative effects on our clients, we mention during our introductions that we work with different horses and, therefore, may switch them at some point during the workshop/seminar/training/event. This way, participants, at least, know the possibility exists. If we do take a horse out, and a particularly strong attachment was formed to this particular horse, we, of course, process that with our clients.

6. Typical Conflict Areas

As your team grows more and more comfortable, many of the recommendations described so far will probably become second nature. You will develop your own style. Let me stress again, there is no right or wrong way for a team to work together, as long as it works for everybody involved. But sometimes, even when we stick to our tried and true tips and tricks, we find ourselves in situations where we suddenly realize there is something going terribly wrong in our team. So, what are the typical topics or conflict areas that come up in equine assisted treatment or corporate teams? How do you know that something is going wrong or that your team is not running as smoothly as it could? And most of all, how, once you have identified the conflict area, do you address, improve or resolve it, especially if you thought your team was foolproof?

6.1.Friendship and Money -- Let's just say: It's complicated....

Supposedly, friendship and money do not mix. This is especially true when financial interests collide with a lack of transparency. Conflict is pre-programmed.

When I started in the EAP business, it was with two riding buddies. It only made sense. We all loved and knew horses and we were together every day anyway. Why not combine our passion with our work? It seemed easy. In fact, we even talked about the money aspect, but we underestimated the amount of time it would take and the lack of money we would make. All this stressed a friendship we thought was solid. Our biggest recommendation is that even if you work with your "bestest buddy", and even if you think there is *no way* money will ever be an issue between the two of you, put everything down in writing. I do not think there is one argument I have not heard from either side – MH or ES – that does not make complete sense yet totally invalidates the other person's point of view. If you write, read, talk about and then sign a contract you agreed on, you have, at least, thought and talked about it, and have that to fall back on. Because, more than likely, if you are friends at the beginning, you will probably end up doing more for each other than you would in a typical work situation. You are probably personally invested as well. Add all this to the initial enthusiasm for finding this type of work which results in countless hours for which you are probably not getting paid and you have the perfect ground for discontent.

The MH, ES and horses have the same importance and value in the team. Our team, therefore, concluded that we should all earn the same amount of money. However, there are a number of reasons why this 1/3 split may not be the optimal solution. For example, different routes to work lead to more gas expenses, something that can not be taken lightly in Europe!!! Differences in time involvement, e.g. pre-session communication with clients; preparation for trainings; follow-ups and feedback rounds after trainings, and different costs for instance for marketing and advertising materials, all related to acquiring new clients are all factors that need to be considered when it comes to splitting up the money. As long as transparency and honesty are present within your team, each problem will have a solution. When all factors are presented, especially if your goal is to continue to work together as a team, you will eventually reach an agreement.

6.2.Liability insurance

Most of us in Europe do not have easy access to insurance companies that have endorsed equine assisted psychotherapy. In the United States, it used to be HUB, an insurance company for horse related activities. Now more and more insurance companies are familiar with equine assisted work that does not involve any riding. The subject of insurance has caused quite a few heated discussions in our team that were not easily resolved. Even though each and every one of our clients signs a liability form, they are fundamentally worthless. We need protection from accidents caused by unintentional negligence on our part. Most Mental Health Specialists have insurance for their therapeutic work. The same goes for consultants and coaches. If they can add that their work involves working with horses, then they are all set. But what type of insurance does the ES need, especially if he is working on a contract basis? Is it sufficient to be insured through your riding business? What if you do not have a riding business? What type of insurance would a private horse owner need who is working with his personal horses? What should your contract look like? Nobody wants or can afford to cover liability suits with their personal property, so it is absolutely necessary that these questions are discussed prior to working with clients. Only when you are no longer concerned about these questions will you be able to put them out of your mind and really focus on your client.

7. Communication, and Communication, and Communication again

7.1.Differences in Communication Styles

Communication is definitely one of my priorities. When I meet new team members, I tell them that I need communication. Lots of it. It is a must and, to me, a plus. But not so for everybody.

In equine assisted teams, it seems like two worlds that could not be any more different come together. On the one side, you have psychotherapists, counselors, educators, etc. whose typical environment is a place where they support and encourage people to TALK. Abstract thinking and theorizing are most comfortable, even desired, and deep thinking about and analysis of events on another level is the norm. There is also, and I hate to say it, most of the time a bit of ego involved when it comes to (my) people from this category. Because let's face it, we are the "Human Specialists".

Then you have the Equine Specialists. In my experience, the really knowledgeable ones support the saying that "Human speech, to horses, is nothing but lip noise." Talking becomes secondary, and most of the good Equine Specialists I know steer away from crowds of people and self-portrayals. They are doers rather than talkers.

Yes, I know I am stereotyping here, but for the sake of simplicity, let's stick to these pictures…

When observing the process between clients and horses, it is important for both team members to share their knowledge and insights. Both parties' knowledge is essential for equine assisted psychotherapy or equine assisted learning to work. There is no preference, no one is better, and there is no competition. What makes equine assisted work so powerful is that it truly is the combined effort of two fields, with the horses as completely impartial parties. Keeping quiet is neither communication nor agreement. Speaking more or louder than someone else does not mean you are right. Any of the above examples can be the first signs of imbalance when it comes to communication.

7.2.Communication and our "Own Stuff"

Many Equine Assisted certification trainings aim to "untrain" people from both categories, in part so that the concept of teamwork may be understood. Why then is there still a minefield for teams to go through when it comes to working together? I think it is because of our own perception, baggage and problems which each one of us brings in.

From the MH's side, the biggest self-contribution is that we are dealing with "our" clients. Depending on where you are working, whether you are paneled with an insurance company or not – you probably have to adhere to licensing rules and regulations and do not want to risk losing your license. Plus, you are probably used to a certain amount of compensation for your work. You have gone to a university to get this degree. You have invested a lot of money into your education. (By the way, is that the money issue again?!) You have practiced, been supervised and mentored, and have a lot of insight-enhancing trainings to justify those additional letters behind your name. I do not know how many times I've heard (or, to be honest, have thought) the statement, "They are *my* patients!" Clinically and ethically, it is the MH's responsibility to determine what intervention is used at what time with what client, and this may look like we are not paying attention to the horses. Seemingly sharing that responsibility or giving some of that to a person who is not trained in clinical skills is very, very difficult[3].

Mental Health Specialists are also used to explaining what we do and looking for underlying reasons, factors and connections. Due to our expertise on human behavior, the inaccurate assumption can be made that we are the overall experts, even when it comes to underlying issues in our team. Add to that a familiarity with transference and counter transference, the psychoanalytical terms for "our own stuff", as well as the ability to put them into words, and the stage is set for any MH to potentially see or be seen as holding a higher position than the ES. Yet any imbalance in the team created by perceived superiorities and inferiorities within the team will undermine efforts to work client centered and remain client focused. Any imbalance in the team due to insecurities and fears associated with increased awareness of "own issues" and self-contributions can be subtle yet will undermine efforts to stay as neutral and "clean[4]" as possible in the interaction with clients. In my experience, it is the awareness of self-contributions that can be the team's biggest asset, but left unaddressed, its presence can become a huge vulnerability and potential area of conflict.

As an ES on our team put it:

"This is a really important point. We – unfortunately – also experienced this in our team. As an ES with tons of experience as a trainer in the business world, I have pretty good self-esteem. Despite that, the first time my MH

---

[3] The "un-training" consists of recognizing that it is not letting go of control but rather listening in a different way.

[4] There are several certifying organizations teaching "clean" language, a concept developed by David Grove in 1980. Clean Language questions are "cleansed as far as possible of anything that comes from the questioner's "maps" -- metaphors, assumptions, paradigms or sensations—that could direct the questionee's attention away from increased awareness of his or her own metaphorical representation of experience".
https://en.wikipedia.org/wiki/Clean_Language (June 2016)

provided me with (I'm trying to be as neutral as possible here) "observations" about a possible self-contribution on my part, it was quite difficult for me. My first impulse was to answer, "Don't you have enough clients to work on? Why can't you just stay out of my head?" Then I stewed over where she got the audacity to dig around and assumed she knew more about me than I did.

I can't remember if I followed through on any of my impulses to tell her how upset I was – but I do know that it took some time for me to start thinking about those "observations" in a less emotional way. Finally, I realized that her observations were not about her having the right to dig around in my head. They were simply so I could ask myself if there was any truth to what she was referring to and, if there was, how it was affecting the work with our clients. That is what it boils down to – being able to work as cleanly as possible with our clients. "My" MH only had that in mind – to ensure that we were providing the best possible care to our clients. That's why, in this line of work, in my opinion, we work not only on our teamwork but also on ourselves."

7.3. Communication, the infamous Self-Contribution, and Being the Boss

As if it is not complicated enough, add "being/having a boss" to the mix. What have we said so far? Two experts – two fields – clients – horses – teamwork. Who decides what needs to be done? Being the boss can throw a wrench into things, especially when the team is trying to see everyone on the same level and of the same importance. Let me get straight to the point. From a business perspective, unless you have a business partnership with all parties equally involved, there is a business owner who needs to make business decisions in addition to everything else. So, even though you are working in a team, possibly with great friends, your position as either the boss or the hired contractor has the potential to exert influence on your perceived roles within your team if you are unable to keep them separate. For example, if you, as the boss, hire somebody, you have the power to fire that somebody. If you get hired, you can also get fired. But how will you reconcile this clear difference in hierarchy between boss and contractor with the idea that, in the arena with clients, everyone is actually the same? Again, there is no right or wrong answer here. Our recommendation is to ask yourself about your team strategy. How do you separate business issues from the team's work? What boundaries do you have? What transparency, what priorities do you have?

8. Possible Suggestions

I believe most team conflicts can be traced back to the listed topics. The visible effects of discrepancies and miscommunication vary: team members talking about each other and splitting apart, voiced disagreement, excuses, unfinished tasks, and an overall lack of trust, …. There are, of course, too many symptoms to list. I strongly support the notion that with an awareness of their self-contribution, any issue or potential conflict area – be it trust, commitment, conflict resolution skills, personality differences, strengths or weaknesses – can be resolved. This is where we're lucky. We work with horses in ways that help people overcome their differences and difficulties! We already facilitate change, so why not go back to our equine team members and let them help us improve our team work as well?

Let me state clearly where I see the power of any equine assisted model that is integrated in proven, evidence-based methods. As human team members, I consider it our job to provide and keep a space for our clients and the horses to interact. That space is to be kept as "clean" as possible – meaning no undue influence from anybody but the client is allowed inside. In this room, the possibility exists for clients and horses to develop their story. It is kind of like a play where the stage and props are provided but the script is only available to the actors. As human facilitators, we watch with curiosity and gear our questions toward understanding what we see, making it possible for our clients to become aware of their behaviors and parts in their own story. Keeping the stage clear of interpretation and our self-contributions opens the door and allows that story to progress and, ultimately, for people to be able to change. When we switch roles and become actors in our own stories, we take on a double role. We get emotionally involved in the process, yet also try to maintain an observer's point of view to help us understand our own part in whatever issue we are working through or decision we are trying to make. Just like our clients, we can develop our own story and build on what we have experienced. I encourage each and every team not only to practice their teamwork, but to work on making it better! Do not take it for granted, and do take care of it. It is worth it.

8.1."Holding Space" vs. "Holding the Frame" (Minds-n-Motion Blog)

It was during an EAGALA training about a year ago when my co-trainer and I discovered that we were speaking about two different things: she was saying "holding space", I was saying "holding the frame". At the time we thought it was a language thing, but upon taking time to reflect about it, it turned out to be two different things.

"Holding the space" for someone is very important, particularly in psychotherapy. It implies to not interfere in a client's process, and how I like to put it, leaving interpretations and pace to process up to the client.

"Holding the frame" is equally important: it means that even though we facilitate a client's process by accompanying him, in equine assisted psychotherapy, we do not lose track of the agreed upon treatment plan and treatment goal, and in corporate work, we do not lose track of the agreed upon and contracted learning goal.

It does not mean that we are goal oriented, but simply that we continue to be clinicians, utilizing various techniques (mainly the horse observations) to facilitate a client's individual process.

Two different things, equally important.

8.2.Getting to know each other....

Before you explore your team dynamics, start with yourself. Not only will it assist you in identifying your assets and weaknesses, but it will also open up lines of communication within your team. This is done best, of course, by taking it to the horses.

Choose a horse that most resembles you and describe the strengths and weaknesses you share. Introduce this horse/yourself to your human team members, then stick with the metaphor of "your" horse as "yourself" throughout the activities for that day, unless otherwise indicated.

Try out different perspectives, e.g. self and teammates' perception: how do I see myself – how do my teammates see me? What strengths/weaknesses do I see in myself, what do they see? Depending on the level of trust and comfort in your team, sharing these impressions can help improve your coordination in the team.

8.3.... And Then Have Fun!

From there, you can pick the area you want to explore. It is trust? Communication? Boundaries? Any other category we have listed in this manual? You know how limitless the human mind is – look at your concerns and explore them with your team!

Typically, we ask clients to set up their topics; meaning – they build and create it. Whatever topic you decide on in your team, build or create it in a way that represents and/or resembles what all of you envision. You might be surprised to see how differently or similarly you and your team members' ideas take shape! Then, explore further. How do you get along with yourself (the horse that most resembles you) - how do you work best with the horses that most resemble your team members? What strengths and weaknesses come into play? How do you overcome, defend and define your boundaries? How do you overcome your struggles and problems?

Explore and experiment with what works for your team and maybe, hopefully, you can enjoy this process of getting to know each other, respecting each other, and learning about each other, to where when you do work with clients you not only facilitate change, but possibly experience the joys of meaningful work!

9. Thank You!

A "thank you" for a great teamwork experience goes to my co-workers Kristel and Sharon – it was a blast! The Belgium EAGALA training in 2012 was the first time we worked together in this constellation.

10. About the Author

Ilka Parent, EAGALA Advanced, EAGALA mentor and former EAGALA Trainer, grew up in Germany, moved to the United States in 1992, and, as of June 2011, resides back in Germany. She earned her Diploma in Psychology in 1997 at the Johannes Gutenberg University in Mainz, Germany, got licensed as LPC and completed her psychoanalytical psychotherapeutic training in Texas. Being married to a military service member afforded her the opportunity to work in various military departments, ultimately in private practice, primarily with active duty service members and their families. On a personal level, she continued both her passion for psychology as well as her passion of working with and training horses. At times, her passion for clinical psychology proved helpful when working with horses, and she often found herself combining both areas. In 2006, she started hearing about EAGALA. Since her initial certification in 2007, Equine Assisted Psychotherapy has become an integral part of her work. Due to 9/11, an already high interest in trauma work was propelled, and she started to develop treatment methods that address combat related PTSD in Armed Forces service members. She has been providing outpatient psychotherapeutic services with a predominant focus on EAP to primarily active duty service members and their families since 2007. Upon her return to Germany in 2011, she completed her German licensure in Clinical Psychotherapy as well as Traumatherapy. She is contracted regularly to provide equine assisted psychotherapeutic interventions to international Armed Forces, particularly the German Armed Forces. Her psychodynamic Equine Assisted Trauma Therapy (pPPT) approach has been scientifically monitored by the Trauma Institute Berlin since 2013.